Presented to

_____

On the occasion of

_____

From

_____

Date

_____

SELECTIONS FROM

WHEN I'M ON MY KNEES

ANITA CORRINE DONIHUE

BARBOUR
PUBLISHING, INC.

© 2000 by Barbour Publishing, Inc.

ISBN 1-57748-718-4

Published by Barbour Publishing, Inc., P. O. Box 719, Uhrichsville, Ohio 44683
http://www.barbourbooks.com

ecpa Member of the
Evangelical Christian
Publishers Association

Printed in China.

SELECTIONS FROM
WHEN I'M ON MY KNEES

Table of Contents

Introduction

"Well, all we can do is pray about it."

Oh, no! I can't believe I said that. Again. All we can do is pray? How short-sighted can I be? Great things happen while I'm on my knees. Forces of heaven are released when one person goes to prayer. The same power that raised my Lord Jesus from the dead is available for my needs.

Thank You that when I bow in prayer, Your Son intercedes. In His purity, He raises each of my petitions to You.

Help me pray within Your will. Guide me to right motives while I pray. Give me faith to release my prayers, to commit them to Your power, Your love, and Your glory.

Remind me often, Lord, that according to Your will, prayer can move mountains, stop rivers, form seasons, and, best of all, change hearts.

Father, here are my concerns and needs. I commit them to You. I thank You in Jesus' name for the answers that will come according to Your will. I trust Your wisdom and give You all the praise.

PART 1

Praise

*Give ear to my words, O LORD,
consider my meditation. . . .
My voice shalt thou hear
in the morning, O LORD;
in the morning will I direct my prayer
unto thee, and will look up.*
PSALM 5:1, 3 KJV

PRAISE YOU FOR HEAVEN

My thoughts often turn toward heaven, Lord. When earthly trials and worries surround me, I long to be with You. I feel homesick, as though I have some subconscious memory of having been in heaven before. Could I have been with You there before I was placed in my mother's womb? Someday I'll have the answers.

I don't feel a part of the evil in this world, and I'm certainly not attracted to what it has to offer. All the money I could earn, the treasure I can obtain, the land I may plan to buy are nothing in light of my eternal home with You. Earthly things lose their value. They wear out, rust, fade, and are sometimes stolen. The eternal treasures I store in heaven with You can never be taken from me. So I'll invest my meager riches in You and Your work. I can't help but love You more than anything the world can give me.

Although my body will die, my soul grows closer to You with each passing day. All the trials and sufferings are minor and won't last. Thank You for the heavenly home I'll go to some day. There will be no sickness there, no pain, no tears. Only eternal life filled with joy and gladness awaits me. There I can be with You and praise You forever.

JOYFUL, JOYFUL,
WE ADORE THEE

Joyful, joyful, we adore Thee.
God of glory, Lord of love;
Hearts unfold like flowers before Thee,
Opening to the sun above.

Melt the clouds of sin and sadness,
Drive the dark of doubt away;
Giver of immortal gladness,
Fill us with the light of day.

Henry Van Dyke

THANK YOU FOR YOUR WONDROUS WORKS

Thank You, Lord, for Your wondrous works and all the things You do for me. I praise You with my whole heart and soul. So many times You shower Your mercy on me and forgive my sins. You reach down and heal my tired body. Your love, mercy, and patience go beyond measure. You help me in my depths of despair and actually pump new life and enthusiasm into me.

I marvel at how You roll out the star-filled sky like a scroll. The oceans look as though You have scooped them out with Your mighty hand. Even the winds and waves are in Your control. You care about the wild birds and animals. How grateful I am that You also care for me.

You are my King of Kings. How I love You, Lord. I will praise You and strive to be a blessing to You forever.

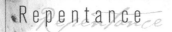

PART 2

Repentance

I will greatly rejoice in the LORD, my soul shall be joyful in my God; for he hath clothed me with the garments of salvation, he hath covered me with the robe of righteousness, as a bridegroom decketh himself with ornaments, and as a bride adorneth herself with her jewels.

ISAIAH 61:10 KJV

12

GOSSIP

I opened my mouth before I thought. Forgive me, Lord. How could I have talked so behind someone's back? I can never retrieve careless words.

Give me strength to ask for forgiveness, to try to make things right. Go before me, dear Lord, and help me make amends.

I am beginning to realize gossip cuts to the core. Wise words soothe and heal. Teach me, Lord, to use words of wisdom, and in the future let me remember the hard lesson from this experience. Guard my tongue and seal my lips. The Bible shows me that careless words can break bones.

May I not get caught in the snares of others who are gossiping. Help me to build up life's cornerstones in people, rather than chiseling and breaking them down.

Fill my thoughts with things that are good and right. Let everything I do and say be pleasing to You.

Now, I focus my eyes on You, dear Lord. I take refuge in Your strength and comfort in Your wisdom.

There is no fear in love.
But perfect love drives out fear,
because fear has to do with punishment.
The one who fears
is not made perfect in love.
We love because he first loved us.

1 JOHN 4:18–19 NIV

Peacemakers who sow in peace raise a harvest of righteousness.
James 3:18 NIV

THE ARGUMENT

ord, I did it again. I fell into another argument and spoke unkindly. Why was I so thoughtless? My heart feels heavy; I find myself replaying the disagreement all day. Can I be wrong although I know I'm "right"?

Is my attitude pure, unconditional love?

Please calm my emotions. Help us to talk, to show respect, and to listen rather than argue.

When I must disagree, help me express my feelings with love, doing my best to keep this person's dignity intact. Show me how to separate the essential from the trivial and to know where I should give in. In spite of our differences, I must remain accepting of the one I love.

Has it been seventy times seven that I have forgiven? Help me show gentleness and forgiveness as You do. Let me be willing not to hold a grudge. Teach me to go beyond myself with thoughtfulness and kindness during this time, remembering that perfect love casts out fear.

Surround me and my loved one with Your presence and keep us nestled in Your pure, sweet love.

*L*inda sputtered at her husband Don and stormed out, angry enough to walk five miles. After a few blocks, her pace lessened. Her racing mind settled. She clutched her sweater with folded arms. Was she cold from the evening air or from chilling words she had spoken? Did it really matter who was right or wrong? Linda thought of how defensive she'd become from her husband's comment. Could it be because there was some truth to what he'd said? She rounded another neighborhood block, afraid to apologize. What if he wouldn't listen? Must she state her view again?

Linda remembered the Bible verse: "Perfect love drives out fear" 1 John 4:18 (NIV). Her conscience gently chided, "There is no need for excuses, just love."

Her pace quickened, and Linda headed for home. When she approached their front yard, she could see the warm glow of living room lights. She quietly opened the door and paused, welcomed by Don's open arms. "I'm sorry," she cried.

"So am I."

"How could I have been so thoughtless?"

"We'll work it out."

"I'll try to understand."

The chill left. Love's warmth returned.

PART 3
Forgiveness

"Forgive and you will be forgiven."
LUKE 6:37 NIV

THANK YOU
FOR YOUR FORGIVENESS

*F*ather, my heart cries out with sorrow and regret for the sin I've committed. How can I possibly forgive myself for such a deed? I know I've hurt You, because You love me so. I try and try to do what is right, but I just mess up time after time. Please forgive me and help me to forgive myself. In Jesus' name.

THE ANSWER

My dear child, what other times?
I've washed all that away with my blood.
Forgive as I forgive you.
Love, Jesus

I Met the Master Face-to-Face

I had walked life's path with an easy tread
Had followed where comfort and pleasure led;
And then one day in a quiet place
I met the Master, face-to-face.

With station and rank and wealth for a goal
Much thought for the body, but none for the soul;
I had thought to win in life's mad race,
When I met the Master, face-to-face.

I had built my castles and reared them high,
Till their towers pierced the blue of the sky,
I had vowed to rule with an iron mace,
When I met the Master, face-to-face.

I met Him and knew Him, and blushed to see
That His eyes full of sorrow were turned on me;
And I faltered, and fell at His feet that day,
While all my castles melted away.

Melted and vanished, and in their place
I saw nothing else but my Master's face;
And I cried aloud: "Oh, make me meet
To follow the path of Thy wounded feet."
And now my thoughts are for souls of men,
I've lost my life, to find it again.
E'er since that day in a quiet place
I met the Master, face-to-face.

Author Unknown

Jesus!
what a friend for sinners!
Jesus!
lover of my soul;
Friends may fail me
foes assail me,
He, my Savior, makes me whole.

J. Wilbur Chapman

No matter how hard she tried, Susan couldn't forgive her daughter Alyssa and her friends for what they had done during their rebellious teenage years. Now an adult, something was keeping Alyssa from living a victorious Christian life. What could it be? Susan prayed for her often but couldn't identify the problem.

The Lord spoke to Susan's heart. He showed her that until she could forgive, she too was in sin. He helped her realize the hurt and anger she felt were linked together, and that she had to let go of both in order to truly forgive. Susan asked God to help her forgive and let go of the painful memories.

The next time Alyssa came to visit, Susan's heart was free from fear, hurt, and bitterness. She and Alyssa took a long walk on a hiking trail shortly before the daughter was to return to her own home. As they walked and visited, Alyssa noticed something different about her mother and asked what it was. The mother told Alyssa how God had helped her change. She assured her daughter of the pride and of the unconditional love she felt for Alyssa. A bond of joy and freedom they hadn't experienced for years returned to mother and daughter. No excuses for shortcomings were offered by either—just "sorries" and forgiveness.

Soon after, Alyssa's love for the Lord matured. Susan felt thankful she was finally able to forgive, love, and step out of God's way, so He could work.

PART 4

Dedication

*May the words of my mouth
and the meditation of my heart
be pleasing in your sight,
O LORD, my Rock and my Redeemer.*
PSALM 19:14 NIV

BALANCING THE BUDGET

*D*ear Father, how can I pay these bills? Sometimes I don't even know where food money will come from. I'm working as hard as possible, but on paper I can't meet the budget.

I give it to You, dear Lord. I place myself and these bills in Your hands and ask for Your direction. Show me how I can help others even while I hurt financially. Help me share a portion of my earnings with You for Your glory. Remind me to give You first place in my pocket book!

Teach me to be prudent in my spending, wise in my financial decisions, and responsible in attempting to pay my obligations.

Enable me to trust You to provide for my needs so I won't worry about food or drink, money or clothes. You already know my needs. I thank You for providing.

Let me not be anxious about tomorrow. I know You will take care of that, too. I will take each day as it comes and commit it to You.

I will trust You, Lord, and not lean on my own understanding of these situations. Instead, with all my might, I will recognize Your will to direct my paths.

GROWING OLDER

Lord, that big zero in my age just rounded the corner. My friends tease me about being over-the-hill. They say the best of life is gone. When I hear this, I laugh.

I wonder what You have in store for me this next year? How can You use me during this phase of my life? I have no fear of growing older. Life is out there to enjoy. Thank You for giving me one more year to do so.

I will not be poured into an ancient mold. I may be growing older, but I refuse to act old. Old age is an attitude. I'm determined to live life abundantly through Your joy and strength.

I see the trees with their scars and burls. Reflecting Your glorious sunset, their branches reach heavenward and praise You, O God. They have survived many of life's storms, just like me. In the still of evening I can hear their rustling boughs whisper a night wind's song, thanking You for life.

I'm not ashamed of pain-filled fingers gnarled from arthritis. They show the work I have done for others. I see the wrinkles collecting on my face. Character lines, I call them. I especially like the ones put there from years of smiles. No matter my health, I can always find ways to serve You, such as letters to the lonely. Best of all, I can hold others up in faithful prayer.

I thank You, Lord, for life, and that You offer it to me in an abundance of spirit and joy. Even as I reach my sunset years, I lift my praise to You. May I reflect Your Holy Spirit all the days of my life.

One of the most difficult things about dedicating our all to God is relinquishing control. We don't know what He has in store for us. We are fearful it may be too difficult or uncomfortable. Often we worry that we won't be able to measure up.

We must remember that God knows our future; He has our concerns and best interests at heart. Along the way we may not understand the reasoning of His direction for us. As we continue walking by faith in the paths He blazes, we'll learn His answers.

Take each step; obey, and fear not. One day, one moment at a time is all He asks. When troubles come, look to Him; plant your feet on His path, and dig in your toes. Don't waver! He'll show the best way. He has already walked the path.

God owns our money,
    our homes.
God owns the land our homes stand on,
    our cars.
God owns our clothes,
    all our treasures.

God wants us to help others,
    our churches.
God wants us to be trustworthy,
    responsible.
God wants us to take care of what we have,
    to submit all and trust in Him.

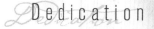

I DEDICATE MY HEART TO YOU

*F*ather, I give You my heart, my soul, my life. I dedicate my whole being to You. I give You my failures and my successes, my fears and my aspirations.

Search my heart. Let my thoughts and motives be pure. You know me through and through. Remove the unclean ways in me that I might be pleasing to You.

Fill me with Your spirit, I pray; enable me to do the tasks set before me. Lead me into Your everlasting way.

Wherever I go, whatever the challenge, I pray that You will be there, guiding me completely. From my rising in the morn to my resting at night, O Lord, be near, surrounding me continually with Your love.

I look forward with joyful anticipation to what You have planned for me. Thank You for becoming Lord of my life.

PART 5

Grief

The grass withereth, the flower fadeth:
but the word of our God shall stand forever.
ISAIAH 40:8 KJV

My Loved One Has Gone

Dear Lord, I miss my loved one so. Since this dear one has died, there's a huge gap in my life. Will it ever be filled? In all this, I thank You for friends and family who show they care. Grant me energy to reach out to them in return and to accept and give love. Perhaps it will help fill some of the emptiness.

Comfort and help me find my way through all of this. Let me recall and cherish the good times, to let the bad memories go.

How can I bear my loss? I long for the one who was so full of life and beauty, like the roses outside my window. My roses will fade from winter's chill, and so, too, have I seen my loved one fade. I gaze at my lovely garden with its splendid array of color. I'm reminded that my dear one who loved You will blossom in full glory for You in Heaven.

I take comfort in Your presence and cling to the assurance that You, the Rose of Sharon, will always abide with me.

LORD, TAKE ME HOME

At times like this, Lord, I can hardly stand all the hurts, tragedies, and sin in this world. I'm forced to brush shoulders with it every day.

It grieves me when loved ones and friends fall away from you, marriages dissolve, and disaster strikes, over and over. What bothers me most is when I see little children suffer from abuse, illness, and neglect. Lord, please take me Home—I'm tired of being here. I feel ashamed to pray this way. But, oh, the pain. Thank You for loving me in my weakest moments.

I read in Your Word when You said, "Not My will, but Thine be done." If you need to keep me here, so be it, dear Lord, although I long to be with You. As long as You have a purpose for me, I will serve You with all my heart. Grant me comfort and strength, I pray. And, Father, when You're finished with me here, I'm ready to come home to You.

TAKE ME HOME

What is this tugging at my heart?
'Tis like a homing dove.
How can I long for a place unseen.
And feel His endless love?

Homesick and worn, I strive each day,
A broken soul to love.
But my broken heart aches to join,
My Savior up above.

How long must I fight the battles,
On tearstained fields for Thee?
"Until your task is finished here,"
He firmly says to me.

"I've covered your scars with my blood.
I've washed your hands and feet.
I've taken the sins of your soul.
To the mercy seat."

What love I feel in His voice,
His hands outstretched to me.
I'll serve until that moment,
His loving face I see.

Grief

Think of stepping on shore and finding it heaven!
Of taking hold of a hand and finding it God's,
Of breathing new air, and finding it celestial air,
Of feeling invigorated, and finding it immortality,
Of passing from storm and tempest to an unbroken
calm,
Of waking up, and finding it home!

Anonymous

MY CHILD IS NOT WHOLE

*D*ear Lord, help my child who isn't whole. Why does my little one have to be this way? Why does such a precious child have these deficiencies? Sometimes I blame myself. If I had done this or that, would it have made a difference? My heart aches, longing for things to be better. I wish I could understand.

I love my child so much. Even though this dear one is disabled, to me I have the most wonderful little one in the world. I thank You for giving me such a sweet gift. Could my child be an angel in disguise?

Grant me patience daily, yet give me determination and consistency. Give me wisdom as I expect my child to do the best that abilities provide, yet let me be realistic in my expectations. Remind me to praise and accent the little accomplishments; help me build self-esteem. Let me cherish each day for the good times. Grant me strength when I am weak and weary, a calm spirit when I am frustrated.

Use this child, I pray, to be a blessing for You and those nearby. Let me learn from my experiences, and let me be of help to others with children who also are not whole.

Thank You, Lord, for giving me my child. Remind me that in Your eyes this little one *is* whole.

PART 6
Healing

But they that wait upon the LORD shall renew their strength;
they shall mount up with wings as eagles; they shall run,
and not be weary; and they shall walk, and not faint.
ISAIAH 40:31 KJV

BURNED OUT

Lord, I let myself get caught up in doing too many things. I'm burned out, so burned out I don't want to go anywhere or do anything. Bitterness and resentment are creeping in. Forgive me, Lord, and heal me. During this time of weakness, let me wait on You. Renew my strength, Lord, that I too can mount like the eagle. Please clip my wings just a little to keep me nearer You, to learn my limitations.

Let me put Your will first in my life, not the will of others. Give me the strength to say, "No thank you," in a loving, but firm way. Help me not to feel guilty. Perhaps I'm cheating others from the chance to serve.

Grant me wisdom in setting the right priorities: You first, my family second, and others next. Somewhere in there show me how to take time for me.

You are the Holy One of my life. I wonder, as You run an entire universe, how can You be concerned with the likes of me? I praise You, O Lord, that You consider me a treasure and that You love me with Your unconditional and everlasting love.

Give me time to mend. In Your own time, send me forth to work again for You. But for now, help me to lie back and absorb Your healing strength.

RESTING IN HIS WAY

When my weary body fails me,
And my mind is filled with strife,
When the world is pressing 'round me,
And I cannot deal with life,

When I've taken on the burdens,
Far more than I should share,
I cry with broken spirit,
"Lord, don't others even care?"

In my darkest midnight hours,
I hear You calmly say,
"You must take My yoke upon you.
You must rest within My way."

Then my many cares I gather,
And I lay them at Your feet.
Where I let Your love surround me,
As my every need You meet.

PICK UP THE BROKEN PIECES

Father, I am broken. I seem to be filled with absolute emptiness. I have nothing to offer You but pieces of my life. Pick them up, I pray, and use them. Help me submit, while You arrange these pieces in a new way. I understand Your way is best. You are the Master Craftsman and know my very being. Thank You for the miracle You create from my shattered life. Thank You for how You are making me into a beautiful new vessel to be used for You. In Jesus' name, I pray.

From birth, Sandra had been abused. No one else knew about it. Physical and emotional hurt became almost unbearable. God helped her. He provided friends who led Sandra to accept Christ as her Savior. Teachers, even strangers, watered the seed of salvation as she grew up.

After high school, Sandra moved away, but couldn't be free from hurt and anger. God helped her again.

One Sunday she went to a nearby church. The people showed her the love she so desperately needed. Sandra's new pastor and wife spent hours of prayer and Bible study with Sandra, and she learned to give hurts and bitterness to God. Yet the pain returned.

Sandra went with some friends to a women's retreat. Between conferences she slipped away to a prayer chapel and met with the Lord again. She told Him she couldn't continue with the hurt and grief any longer. In the chapel, God reminded Sandra He was her heavenly Father; that He loved the fragile little girl within her. Sandra felt like He reached down and wrapped His arms around her—she knew He listened and took them all on His shoulders.

Although the past would never be right, Sandra accepted God's comfort and healing. She found peace. When pain and bad memories returned, she gave them back to the Lord, her Healer and heavenly Father.

PART 7
Trials

*But the LORD is my defence;
and my God is the rock of my refuge.*
PSALM 94:22 KJV

SINGING IN THE STORMS

The storms of life surround me, but I will not be tossed to and fro. I am anchored in Your steadfast love. A song of praise wells up from my heart. I will sing praise and glory to Your name while You carry me through this, another storm. You alone know the answers and the outcome. I take comfort in Your mighty presence.

I turn into the wind, unafraid, ready to face each day head on, flanked with Your power and wisdom. In the peak of the storm, when I feel I can hold on no longer, I will call on Your name for peace. I will trust in You and will not feel afraid, as I nestle into Your protecting hands.

How is it that You have such mighty power, that the tempests in my life cease their crashing winds at Your command? How is it that You can calm my raging seas of circumstances and emotions and bring my life into Your control with Your powerful, yet hushed voice?

Even now, I hear Your whisper, "Peace, be still. Know I am your God."

When the storm subsides, my song of praise for You will echo throughout the ages from generation to generation, telling of Your mighty works and deeds.

Thank You, dear Lord, for Your help and peace.

> *. . .and underneath*
> *are the everlasting arms. . .*
> DEUTERONOMY 33:27 KJV

*T*wo years ago, Dad and I took a trip to Quebec. Armed with video camera, munchies, and suitcases, we headed out.

We found Quebec to be charming and lovely, but the little French we knew made following directions challenging. One night we had a motel reserved outside Montreal. The big city traffic and a storm warning for early afternoon concerned me. We planned to reach our destination by 3:00 P.M.

As we approached the outskirts of Montreal, we came onto major road construction. Exit signs had been removed, and we missed our turnoff and ended up in downtown Montreal. I couldn't get us back to where we belonged. Time ticked away to 3:30. Rush hour traffic and the predicted storm came.

I strained to focus through rapid windshield wipers and the worst torrent of rain I'd ever seen. Gushing water prevented any vision beyond the hood of the car. There was no place to pull off and park. We had to keep moving! Trucks flew by on both sides, bathing the little car. Dad dug out his camera, recording the action. He always loved a storm.

"Hey!" shouted Dad. "I can see clearly through this camera. It's like a filter."

I trusted Dad as he calmly directed me. We reached a traffic jam in a nearby tunnel. We stopped and I slumped over the wheel. I tried to appear calm for Dad's sake, but I was almost in tears.

Please, Lord, I prayed. *Move the storm and help us find our way.* Traffic slowly edged on. The song, "Wonderful Grace of Jesus" whirred through my mind like a revolving tape. We approached the tunnel's opening and the sheet of rain. I nosed the car out. At the same time, a gust of wind moved the storm to our right like the parting of the Red Sea. Before long we made it to our destination.

Trials

*A*t times I find myself struggling and losing my way. I end up in one of life's storms. Then I remember Montreal. God doesn't always move or end the storms, but He calms my spirit, and He gives me a song for courage. Just like Dad's camera filtered through the rain, God filters through my problems. As I obey Him and read His word, He guides me along life's freeways.

Thou are my hiding place;
thou shalt preserve me from trouble;
thou shalt compass me about
with songs of deliverance.

PSALM 32:7 KJV

PART 8
Deliverance

God has said,
"Never will I leave you;
never will I forsake you."
So we say with confidence,
"The Lord is my helper;
I will not be afraid. . . ."
HEBREWS 13:5–6 NIV

I DON'T LIKE MY JOB

*Be of good
courage,
He shall
strengthen
you.
Hope
in the Lord;
He will see
you through.*

*D*ear Father, I pray You will help me with my job. Things aren't going right. I dread going to work and I need Your direction. On days I feel I'm doing more than my share, may my attitude be right. Give me wisdom, I pray. When I do menial tasks, help me remember when Your Son, though King of Kings, came down from heaven and often acted as a servant. Let me not be too proud to serve.

Help me to be honest in estimating my own abilities, to not put myself down or become a braggart. Teach me to appreciate a job well done, to feel an inner sense of accomplishment. I lean on You, not only on my skills. I know I can earn my pay and make a living; or I can give of myself and make a life.

Go before me when there is friction and backbiting. Let my motives be pure and uplifting, depending on Your help, so Your light can shine through.

FROM CALAMITY TO CALM

*F*ather, this day has too much responsibility for me. My head spins with frustration. My life is full of calamity. Help me to gain Your perspective. When my footing begins to slip, let me cling to You, my Fortress. Instill Your direction in my cluttered mind. When I am weak, lend me Your quiet, confident strength; when impatient, grant me Your patience. If I fail, help me not to keep punishing myself, but to leave it in Your hands and go on.

Teach me to eliminate those things that are unnecessary and to concentrate on the essentials. Help me slow down enough to take time for myself and You.

Keep my thoughts accurate, my hands sure, and my feet swift in doing Your will. Remind me of my limitations, Lord. Keep my step close behind— not in front of—You and protect me with Your strong hands.

At the day's end, I will lie down and reflect on all I have learned. I will recall how much You have helped me. I will praise You with great joy as I drift to sleep, nestled in the protection of Your mighty wings.

I will instruct you and
teach you in the way you should go;
I will counsel you and watch over you.

Psalm 32:8 NIV

It's easy in our fast-paced world to let life control our schedules. Before long, we find our days filled with jumble, wasted time, an overabundance of television, senseless actions, going nowhere. Like spinning wheels on a slippery freeway, we lose our spiritual footing, become irritable and frustrated. Our songs of praise and worship (when we listen to them) ring in our ears like fast-forward recordings. No concept. No application. No direction.

We need to pull off life's fast lane for awhile and turn to God for direction and strength. Let's tune in to His voice and marvel as He prepares the way for us. As we seek His direction, He miraculously makes more time in our day. Then at night, we can look back and be satisfied within His will.

PART 9
Family

*"But as for me and my household,
we will serve the LORD."*
JOSHUA 24:15 NIV

OUR NEWBORN BABY

Look at our beautiful baby, Lord, at these tiny fingers wrapped around mine. Look how this darling rests securely in my arms. See Daddy's proud gaze. Already my heart overflows with love. I talked to and prayed for this sweet one even while the baby was yet still in my womb.

What does our baby's future hold? Prepare the way that our child may grow up to love and serve You. Grant my husband and me wisdom in raising such a precious gift.

Today, O Lord, I dedicate our baby as a love offering to You. Like Hannah in days of old, I thank You for giving our little one to us. Here and now, I present our child at Your altar to be raised for Your service.

Let Your angels encamp around and about, and protect from evil and harm.

> *"Many women do noble things, but you surpass them all."*
>
> PROVERBS 31:29
> NIV

Help us teach Your ways by truth and example. When we err, I pray, dear Lord, that You will help meet the needs and forgive us. Place Christians in life's pathway. I pray that You will create a special hunger in this little heart to know, love, and serve You completely.

Help me remember our child is lent to us for a little while and that You are the Lender. Let me not take our dear one back from You or pursue my own ways outside Your will.

I will bless Your name, O Lord, thanking You for this wonderful infant gift. I praise Your name in my thoughts, motives, and actions forever.

THANK YOU
FOR THIS SPECIAL DAY

Lord, I collapse onto our couch, kick my shoes off, and think of today's blessings. Family and friends bustled around. Children chattered with youthful excitement. Steaming irresistible foods simmered in the kitchen. Men exchanged stories and (thank You, Lord) helped with the little ones. It seems a whooshing dream; the day went so fast.

I reflect briefly on the struggles we've all had, the mountains we've fearfully conquered with Your help. Still we're together, loving and sharing. It was worth listening to each other and finding Your will through the years.

I'm tired, but I loved it all. At nightfall, little arms wrapped around my neck with an "I love you, Nana." Strong embraces from sons so dear and tender hugs from loving daughters filled my heart with joy. When did I earn such love and honor? I don't know, but I thank You for it, Lord. I treasure the look of pleasure and pride, the squeeze of a hand from my own dear parents.

Now the silence is here, ringing its tranquil melody. I lean over and nuzzle my head on my husband's shoulder. His look is one of fulfillment and approval. Love softly drifts between us.

I thank You, Lord, for this day that You created and for the love of family and friends.

As special days end in all their wild flurry, I'm often reminded of the true value in it all: not food, fancies, and elaborations, but my dearest friends and loved ones.

*She watches over
the affairs of her household
and does not eat the bread of idleness.
Her children arise and call her blessed;
her husband also, and he praises her.*

PROVERBS 31:27–28 NIV

BLESS THROUGH GENERATIONS

Father, in this uncertain world filled with danger and turmoil, I ask You to protect my family.

Will I live to see my children grown? Will I live to see my grandchildren? My great-grandchildren? I can only trust and make each day count for something.

Forgive us for providing such a world as this with all its problems. Yet I praise You for the many good things that are available to my children.

Lord, please bless my family for generations to come. May the Christian teachings we instill be passed from one generation to the next. Grant each dear one wisdom and strength.

Can it be that my simple prayers for them will be generated by Your power, the same power released when Your Son died on the cross and rose again? Will these prayers be made ageless? I take comfort that when I am gone, my prayers will continue into eternity with You, Lord Jesus, interceding on behalf of each one.

Just as You prayed for me in the garden of Gethsemane, I am assured that You accept my prayers for these, my children, my children's children, and on through the generations. I have no fear for their future, because I place them in Your loving care. Thank You for Your peace.

PART 10

A friend loveth at all times. . . .
PROVERBS 17:17 KJV

THANK YOU FOR THE MAN I LOVE

He gazes at me from across the packed room. We're at just another meeting, but I dressed to look my best. Do I see the same twinkle in his eyes I saw when we first met? Do I see the same look he wore on our wedding day? Am I so blessed that he still gazes at me with the same love and pride? Thank You, Lord, for that look. Thank You for today and for him.

Help me show to him the same love and thoughtfulness as when we first married. In our hurried schedules, let us look for time to spend with each other. Sometimes I love even sharing a second glass of iced tea on the patio at sundown.

I think of changes we've faced and will continue to experience. We have fallen in love with each other over and over again, even while changing.

Teach us to keep respecting one another's feelings. Teach us to put each other first, after You.

And, Lord, help me keep myself in a way that he will always look across the room with love and pride.

And now these three remain:
faith, hope and love.
But the greatest of these is love.

1 CORINTHIANS 13:13 NIV

ove? I will tell you what it is to love!
It is to build with human hearts a shrine,
Where hope sits brooding like a beauteous dove,
Where time seems young, and life a thing divine.

Charles Swain

THANK YOU FOR MY FRIEND

She was there, again, right when I needed a listening ear and a shoulder to lean on. Thank You for my friend, Lord. She is so special to me. Whenever we can't see each other, there are little thought waves going back and forth between us and little "arrow prayers" going up for one another during the day.

Thank You for my friend when she brings over a tray of cookies and I pour the tea. Amidst the work, our world stops while we take a little time for each other's company.

Help me never to take my friend for granted but to treat her with thoughtfulness. Help me to recognize when she wants my company and when she needs time alone.

I know we will remain close friends for many years to come. For every year we have, I am thankful.

PART 11

God's Faithfulness

O LORD God of hosts,
who is a strong LORD like unto thee?
or to thy faithfulness round about thee?
PSALM 89:8 KJV

THE REBELLIOUS CHILD

Father, help my rebelling child. I am overwhelmed with worry. Have I raised this child, once little and carefree, to have this happen? Will my dear one's mistakes cause a lifetime of suffering? Is it all or partly my fault?

Forgive me, O Lord, for the wrongs I have caused my dear child. Let me humble myself and ask this loved one's forgiveness. Let me offer no excuses. Cleanse my heart from bitterness and give me a pure, unconditional love. Grant me wisdom. Teach me when to be lenient, when to be firm. Help me that my motives will be pure, honest, and aboveboard. Remind me often not to try fixing things.

Place Your angels about my child. Protect from sin and harm, and lead to Your perfect will. Soften our hearts. Give us both a hunger to love and serve You.

Now, dear Lord, I release control of my beloved child to You. I will trust You in every situation and timing. Even when I don't understand why, still will I trust and praise You. Through these troublesome times I know You are helping and keeping my dear one in Your care.

Thank You for victories to come. Thank You for hearing my prayers. Thank You that You can go places with my child that I can't. As the answers to prayer come, may I write them down and remember them. Praise You, O God, for Your mighty works. In You I put my total trust.

"Blessed is the man who trusts in the LORD,
whose confidence is in him.
He will be like a tree planted by the water
that sends out its roots by the stream."
JEREMIAH 17:7–8 NIV

God's Faithfulness

*M*y husband Bob and I have five sons, now fine grown men. When we reflect on their teenage years, we recall many happy memories, but also some frightening moments.

During the rebellious, emotional times we discovered valuable lessons. First, we learned to hold a steady, consistent course so our kids could have something stable to look toward. If we strayed in the slightest, it magnified in our children. They challenged everything we said and did.

As our children attempted to find their own way, they tested us for purity and validity. No amount of speeches or attempts to set them straight worked. Communication, listening, and love helped most. We also soon discovered our example meant much more than mere words.

Another lesson learned was to maintain a close fellowship with our Lord. He was our Guide, our Counselor, Friend, and source of strength. Because of this, we were able to give and regive each child to God. He could go with them where we couldn't and speak to each one when our words didn't reach them.

Now we praise God for His miracles and answered prayers and for our beloved family. We still hold those six-foot sons, our precious daughters by marriage, and now our grandchildren up to God and leave them in His care each day.

FATHER, HEAR THE PRAYER WE OFFER

Father, hear the prayer we offer;
Not for ease that prayer shall be,
But for strength that we may ever
Live our lives courageously.

Not forever in green pastures
Do we ask our way to be,
But the steep and rugged pathway
May we tread rejoicingly.

Not forever by still waters
Would we idly quiet stay,
But would smite the living fountains
From the rocks along the way.

Be our strength in hours of weakness;
In our wanderings be our guide;
Through endeavor, failure, danger,
Father, be Thou at our side. Amen.

Love M. Willis

PART 12

Challenge

*However, I consider my life
worth nothing to me,
if only I may finish the race and
complete the task
the Lord Jesus has given me—
the task of testifying to
the gospel of God's grace.*
ACTS 20:24 NIV

LET MY ROOTS SINK DEEP

Lord, I sit alone by a quiet stream. My thoughts turn to Psalm 23. The waters gently ripple by. Trees gracefully bow their branches and teasingly rustle their leaves in the pure, fresh breeze. A bird lilts a beckoning call to its mate. A distant falcon pierces the air with its echoing screech.

Peace. Thank You, Lord. But what about when I must return to the hustle and bustle? How can I be prepared?

I look at the trees; their roots sink deep by the stream. In the same way, let my roots sink deep into You. Let me feed on Your Word. As we commune in prayer, let me drink from the living water of Your spirit. Let me jump in and be bathed by Your cleansing power. I will rely on You rather than things that are shallow and temporary. I can't depend on my own abilities and strength, but I'm confident in Your care and direction.

I will take special notice of the good things when they come. I will fix my mind on what is pure and lovely and upright.

When the heat and winds of life's storms come, I will not fear; I know You are near. I will not worry but keep on producing a life that is a blessing for You and others.

Let me take time often to come drink from Your quiet stream. I thank You for it.

PRAISING GOD FROM THE PITS

Lord, I want to praise You from the pits. Not the pits of self-pity, but the pits carefully placed in the heart of life's race track. I don't have time to feel sorry for myself. I'm in the middle of a race for You.

Each time I round the bend, I trust You to run me through Your checklist to see if I'm in alignment and synchronized to Your will.

I know there are others watching me, but I also know You are helping me discard things and habits that would inhibit me.

I want to praise You as I run with determination. I will put forth every ounce of strength. At times I'm scorned and tested. Other times I'm tempted to take a side path, but I will keep my eyes turned to You, my Creator, the very Being of my faith. I remember how You were scorned, how You were tempted, how You shed Your blood and died on the cross for me.

So when I am weary, lift my hands that I might praise You from the pits. Strengthen my arms, I pray. Keep my feet swift and sure. Make each day's path level before me. My life, I give to You. With all my being, I run this race for You.

NEVER GIVE UP

When you
> believe you're crushed, you are.
> defy not the odds, you lose.
> claim not the victory, you fail.
> settle for one goal, you grow stagnant.

But when you
> learn from the struggles, you resolve.
> ignore the put-downs, you grow.
> choose success, you soar.
> believe in yourself, you gain confidence.
> accept Christ, you gain strength.
> toil unceasingly, you achieve.
> press on, you are enriched.
> fall and start over, you win.

When you do all this, you shall gain life's prize.

I Want to Leave My Mark for You

I know not what each day holds, or what time I have left to serve. This I do know, dear Lord, I want to leave my mark for You.

Help me make every day count. Remind me to lay aside my own wants, to be willingly inconvenienced and used for You. Let me not put anything before You, no matter how good it seems. Help me shed bad habits that slow me down from doing Your will.

I can only leave my mark for You by replacing idle time with purposeful movement. When I rest, I open my heart that You may fill me with Your strength and spirit.

Teach me to let go of yesterday, live fully today, and look with excitement toward tomorrow. I am awed as I daily come to know You more. I feel You shower love upon me like a refreshing summer rain.

Even though I am unworthy, I long to reach the end of life's journey and see You face-to-face. In the meantime, Lord, may I use each day, each hour, each moment to leave my mark for You. Amen.

PART 13

Worship

The grace of the Lord Jesus Christ,
and love of God,
and the communion of the Holy Ghost,
be with you all. Amen.
2 CORINTHIANS 13:14 KJV

THE OCEANS OBEY YOU

Oh Lord, You are mightier than the huge breakers crashing against the ocean rocks. No other is greater than You! You display Your faithfulness in the cycle of the tides. How magnificent is the way their waves rise and fall at Your command. You shout and they rise. You whisper, and they drift softly back into the ocean's depths. How do You cause the waters to stop at the shore? This water, soft as silk and harder than bricks, obeys Your will.

I walk along the sandy beach. I gaze out over the deep waters and recall the turbulence in my own life. Thank You for bringing my storms under control. Your mighty hand snatched me out of trials and tribulations; You have never dropped me.

As I stand gazing at Your marvelous creation, I dig my toes in the sand. The strong wind whips my hair. My tongue savors the salty air. I breathe deeply. Clean, cool air fills my lungs. Your refreshing Spirit surrounds me. You honor me with Your presence. I tremble at the thought of Your greatness.

Thank You for Your creation. Thank You, God, for life.

BE STILL

"Be still," I hear Him softly say.
"Be still, lay all aside."
He who made the universe stoops down
and gathers up my cares.

"Be still," He chides again.
His work begins within my weary soul.
"Be patient. In quiet stay.
Listen to me."

Though pressed on every side,
I clear my heart and mind.
In timid voice and heart,
I lift to Him my praise.

How quiet, His presence.
How healing, His words.
In hushed awe, I listen.
I savor each one.

My will, He bends.
My heart, He sweeps clean.
My strength, He renews.
My soul, He fills to overflowing.

He teaches through His word.
I heed what He tells me.
I stand and give Him praise.
Together we go forth to serve.

JOY OF THE LORD

I look to You, Jesus. Your Promises are true. I look to You, Lord Jesus, You always see me through.

My days are long and weary. My strength is almost gone. I lift my eyes to You, O Lord, my joy and strength. My heart quickens. New energy surges through my body. Gladness fills my heart as I concentrate on You.

Thank You for helping me focus on You, Lord, rather than the negative things in life. When the tasks I have to accomplish seem impossible, thank You for pumping new life into me. Truly, Lord, Your joy is my strength.

As I go about my duties, may Your joy radiate through me. Let Your light shine in me, Your servant, because of the good works You have done. I sing praises and am blessed with Your strength.

Only temporary happiness comes from this world. I take heart in Your joy, the joy of the Holy Spirit. It is indescribable, straight from heaven! Your joy covers suffering, trials, sadness, and exhaustion.

When I experience it, my cup overflows. There is no situation so difficult I cannot overcome with pure, refreshing joy and strength from You. You refresh, cleanse, and comfort, exhilarate and encourage.

I rejoice again and again! You, Lord, stoop from Your throne in heaven, reach down, and nourish me with the Water of Life. You wipe away my tears and replace them with gladness anew and Your pure, sweet joy.

Sing to the LORD a new song,
>his praise in the assembly of the saints.
Let Israel rejoice in their Maker;
>let the people of Zion be glad in their King.
Let them praise his name with dancing
>and make music to him with tambourine and
>harp.
For the LORD takes delight in his people;
>he crowns the humble with salvation.
Let the saints rejoice in this honor
>and sing for joy on their beds.

PSALM 149:1–5 NIV

PART 14

In His Name

*For unto us a child is born,
unto us a son is given:
and the government shall be upon his shoulder:
and his name shall be called Wonderful, Counsellor,
The mighty God, The everlasting Father,
The Prince of Peace.*
ISAIAH 9:6 KJV

EVERLASTING FATHER

What a loving Father You are, my God. Because we couldn't comprehend Your love, You showed us what kind of a Father You are by sending us Your Son.

I bow before You in reverence and fear. The only way I can approach Your throne is through Your Son, Jesus Christ. He has taken away my sins by shedding His priceless blood. This way, You can look upon me, Your unworthy child.

Thank You for loving me. From You came my very being. In You is my course of life. You know my needs, my abilities, my longings. You listen to my joys, my sadness, my frustrations, my dreams. You are my everlasting Father. Thank You for always being present with me. When I call on Your name, I praise You for already being here.

Peace I leave with you,
my peace I give unto you:
not as the world giveth, give I unto you.
Let not your heart be troubled,
neither let it be afraid.

JOHN 14:27 KJV

PRINCE OF PEACE

Praise You for peace, Lord. Not the uncertain peace the world offers, but a peace of heart and mind that only comes from knowing You, the Prince of Peace.

May the rich exalt You and put You first. May the needy lift You up in praise. May all experience true peace and the fullness of life with You as Savior and Lord.

Thank You for Your tender care. Your compassion never fails. During the happy times, may Your guiding presence and peace be acknowledged. In the sad times of want, sickness, or death, still may Your comfort and peace be felt.

Although we are of the world, thank You for Your power to overcome life's overwhelming problems. What a precious gift, Your love and peace. It isn't fragile or fluffy or temporary as the world gives, but deep, satisfying, and dependable, because it comes from You, Almighty God. You are the Prince of Peace. The greatness of its source is more than our finite minds can comprehend.

In all circumstances, I shall not be troubled or afraid. I believe in the Father and I believe in You, my Prince of Peace. I praise You, Lord, with all my heart, mind, and soul. No matter what happens, I accept Your peace, and I will put my trust in You.

EMMANUEL, GOD WITH US

*E*mmanuel, I praise You for promising me You will never leave me nor forsake me. You are my Father, my Helper, my Guide. I shall never fear, for I know You are with me. Thank You for protecting me wherever I am, day and night.

You fill me with strength and courage. When troubles come, others may flee, but You stand by me: my dearest Friend, my Savior.

I praise You for being with me always, even through the end of my earthly life. You, Lord, are the One who died for my sin, yet You live forevermore.

Thank You for always being with me and letting me be with You. Thank You for Your wonderful peace that passes all understanding.

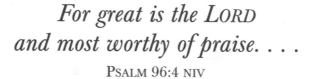

For great is the LORD
and most worthy of praise. . . .

PSALM 96:4 NIV

"In the desert prepare the way for the LORD;
make straight in the wilderness a highway
for our God.
Every valley shall be raised up,
every mountain and hill made low;
the rough ground shall become level,
the rugged places a plain.
And the glory of the LORD will be revealed,
and all mankind together will see it.
For the mouth of the LORD has spoken."

ISAIAH 40:3–5 NIV

SAVIOR

ord, You are my Savior, my Rescuer, Deliverer. Words seem inadequate to praise You for how You saved me from my sins.

How was it possible for You to be born as a man and yet still be the Son of God? You are greater than the angels. You extend Your Father's love to earth and glorify His name. What love You showed when You gave up Your glory in heaven long enough to become a poor child, growing up, loving and serving, and finally laying down Your life. While You lived on earth, You didn't even have a pillow to put Your head on.

All You did for us made it possible for me to have a joyful abundant life through You. Thank you for being my Savior and for allowing me to be Your servant.

THE POTTER

Lord, it makes no difference what comes my way. What really matters is for me to be within Your will. Help me become soft and pliable so You can mold me the way You know I should be.

The potter's wheel spins 'round and 'round. Gentle fingers form the soft clay into the master's desired creation. To the potter, there is purpose in each turn.

At times my life seems to be spinning. Slow me down, Lord. You are the Potter of my life. Let me heed to Your molding so I can be a product of Your perfect plan.

Does not the potter have the right to make out of the same lump of clay some pottery for noble purposes and some for common use?

ROMANS 9:21 NIV

I SING THE ALMIGHTY POWER OF GOD

I sing the almighty power of God,
That made the mountains rise;
That spread the flowing seas abroad,
And built the lofty skies.
I sing the wisdom that ordained
The sun to rule the day;
The moon shines full at His command,
And all the stars obey.

I sing the goodness of the Lord,
That filled the earth with food;
He formed the creatures with His word,
And then pronounced them good.
Lord, how Thy wonders are displayed,
Where'er I turn my eye;
If I survey the ground I tread,
Or gaze upon the sky!

There's not a plant or flower below,
But makes Thy glories known;
And clouds arise, and tempests blow,
By order from Thy throne;
While all that borrows life from Thee
Is ever in Thy care
And everywhere that man can be,
Thou, God, are present there. Amen.

Isaac Watts

A PSALM OF DAVID

O LORD our Lord, how excellent is thy name
    in all the earth! who hast set thy glory above the heavens.
When I consider thy heavens, the work of thy fingers,
    the moon and stars, which thou hast ordained;
What is man, that thou art mindful of him?
    and the son of man, that thou visitest him?
For thou has made him a little lower than the angels,
    and hast crowned him with glory and honour.
Thou madest him to have dominion over the works of thy hands;
    thou has put all things under his feet:
O LORD our Lord, how excellent is thy name
    in all the earth!

Psalm 8:1, 3–6, 9 KJV

CREATOR

*P*raise be to You, O God, my Creator, the source of my entire existence. You were here in the beginning. You were present when there was nothing—no form, only darkness. At Your mighty command there was light. It must have been quite a sight to view the streaks of light shooting across the darkness, dividing nothingness into timely submission. Thank You for how You put light into my life, dispelling darkness and sin.

You created water and land, the sun, moon, and stars. You made creatures of all kinds. Wisdom and balance are rolled from Your fingertips. Then You created man and woman. Some of Your creation gives You joy. Others cause grief. How I pray to reflect You and give You joy, gladness, and pride for having me as Your child.

Your Word says when You completed Your creation, You looked at it and said it was good. May I always make You feel pleased that You created me, Lord. May I spend my life giving honor and glory to You.

Praise be to You, O God, my Creator.

Rejoice, O my soul.
Let all that is within me
praise the Almighty God.

MIGHTY GOD

You are so great, O Mighty God. There is no other like You. I praise You will all my heart and soul. All You are and all You create show splendor and majesty. You unfold the morning skies like a holy robe. You furl it again through the universe at evening to expose the vast starlit heavens. The waters reflect Your glorious rays.

I stretch out on the grass and gaze at the clouds as they play tag like huge, animated animals. The wind blows as though Your forceful breath pushes each cloud with huge gusts. Thunder and lightning put on a dramatic display like a vigorous chariot race.

You, Mighty God, created the mountains in all their grandeur, once covered with gushing waters. At Your command, the waters left and formed rivers in the valleys below. Geysers shoot up; mountains tremble; mud and lava fill once-clear rivers. Some waters even go dry. It all is so fearful. The very balance of nature is threatened, but You have control. Through it all, the earth is purged of disease. The mountains have bellowed out ash that feeds our soil. New green sprouts and lush grass grow. The animals and people return, and life begins anew.

In the same way, You shook my life and cleansed me of impurities. Little by little, You created new growth in me that is fresh and pleasing to You.

How can the birds know where to make such perfect nests? How do they know where to migrate? You planned it for them, mighty God. How amazing! How wonderful! You provide creeks and ponds in pastures for the animals. The cattle come out by day, the wild animals by night to drink.

You give us grains, vegetables, and fruits that seed and reseed themselves. You even planned seasons so all can rest through the winter. In spring, nature awakens and new life begins.

How important are Your works, O Lord. In Your wisdom You have made each one. I will sing praise to Your name. I will meditate on Your good works and rejoice in Your great love.

*F*or the LORD gives wisdom,
    and from his mouth come knowledge and understanding.
He holds victory in store for the upright,
        he is a shield to those whose walk is blameless,
            for he guards the course of the just
                and protects the way of his faithful ones.
                Then you will understand what is right
                    and just and fair—
                    every good path.
                        For wisdom will enter your heart,
                        and knowledge will be pleasant
                            to your soul.

PROVERBS 2:6–10 NIV

JEHOVAH

Jehovah, I give You honor and glory. I trust You with my life. I can always depend on You. Thank You for Your unfailing love. You are trustworthy and sure. In every situation Your promises are sure. You are truth and righteousness. In You, there is no fault.

How virtuous are Your ways. Your laws and directions are upright and perfect. In You, I rely and place all my confidence. You are my King, bold and sure. You faithfulness and love never sway.

Thank You for Your care. Praise be to You, Jehovah, Most High, my God, my Savior.

That men may know that thou, whose name alone is JEHOVAH, art the most high over all the earth.

PSALM 83:18 KJV

GUIDE ME,
O THOU GREAT JEHOVAH

Guide me, O Thou great Jehovah;
Pilgrim through this barren land;
I am weak, but Thou art mighty,
Hold me with Thy powerful hand;
Bread of heaven, Bread of heaven,
Feed me till I want no more,
Feed me till I want no more.

Open now the crystal fountain,
Whence the healing stream doth flow;
Let the fire and cloudy pillar
Lead me all my journey through;
Strong Deliverer, strong Deliverer,
Be Thou still my strength and shield,
Be Thou still my strength and shield.

William Williams

THE WAY, THE TRUTH, AND THE LIFE

At times, Father, my ways haven't been Your ways. After I strayed from Your path, I slipped and fell, soon realizing what disaster I'd gotten myself into. Then with Your help, I struggled to faltering feet and got back on the right course. Then You gave me direction and sound judgment. Thank You for being my Way.

You gave me Your Word. In it, You show me truth, and through Your truth I've been set free. Day by day I study Your Scriptures. Your Word helps me know right from wrong. Through Your Holy Spirit, it advises me in making wise decisions. It cautions me against sinful traps. Thank You for being my Truth.

Because of Your certain way and guiding truth, You lead me into joyous, abundant life. When circumstances are difficult and unsure, I still have a deep inward joy filled with victory only You can provide. Not only do I experience a victorious life here on earth, I look forward to life eternal with You in heaven. Thank You, Lord, for my life.

Track	Title	Time	© ℗
1	To Be in Your Presence	3:12	(1)
2	Worship and Adore	3:10	(2)
3	Praise to the Lord	2:48	(2)
4	The Lord's Prayer	3:30	(1)
5	Break Me Lord	2:39	(2)
6	Come and Bow Before the King	2:23	(2)
7	I Will Seek Your Face	5:13	(1)
8	How Majestic Is Your Name	3:12	(2)
9	Lord, You Have My Heart	3:57	(1)
10	Draw Me Lord	2:33	(2)

TOTAL RUNNING TIME (32:44)

Copyright and Permissions
1–Kingsway Music LTD
2–Classic Fox Records LTD